GOOD GRIEF,

I HAVE TO PLAN A FUNERAL

GOOD GRIEF,

I HAVE TO PLAN A FUNERAL

A Detailed Guide To Planning A Funeral
by
JUDY SMITH ROSS

Illustrations by Beverley Smith

Canadian Cataloguing in Publication Data

Smith Ross, Judy, 1944 –
Good Grief, I have to plan a funeral,
a detailed guide to planning a funeral..

ISBN # 0-9697577-3-5

Illustrations and design – Beverley Smith
Beverley is an illustrator and artist living in Duncan, south of Clarksburg. wwwholycrowbeads.com

Editor – Kathleen Fraser

Title – Liz Grogan

Valley Girls Publishing
Thornbury, Ontario
Printed in Canada by Transcontinental

1st printing December 2004
2nd printing April 2005
3rd printing February 2006

Special Thanks to:

Billy Skwarchuk, Funeral Director
Skwarchuk Funeral Home, Bradford, ON

Michael C. Fawcett, Funeral Director
Fawcett Funeral Home, Collingwood, ON

The Reverend Patt Nunn
Christ Church, Port Stanley, ON

The Reverend Doug Norris
Rosedale United Church, Toronto, ON

This book is in memory of those whose services
provided the material for the book

Thank you to my family and friends who believed not only
in me, but also in the importance of the book.

*"Well Done! Finally an effective manual through the
inevitable. Ultimately, misconceptions and unanswered
questions are clarified through this well documented, soundly
researched guide. A useful tool for everyone."*
Michael Fawcett, Funeral Director.

*" __a fine contribution to the elusive task of preparing for
what we resist being prepared for, and getting through what
so often feels like it cannot be gotten through. I refer to the
Honouring/ Grieving ritual as one of the most Beautiful/ Awful
things we do. You have offered us food for the journey - this
will, I have no doubt, be a blessing and I look forward to
seeing it in print."*
The Reverend Doug Norris.

*"How lucky for all of us that Judy is at last sharing her
experience in funeral planning. As an author, I respect her
research and attention to detail. As an educator, I
appreciate her clear guidelines and sound suggestions. As
a friend, I thank her for guiding me effortlessly through
three difficult funerals. Let her do the same for you."*
Ellen Bear, Author, Educator.

TABLE OF CONTENTS

INTRODUCTION

When a friend's father died recently, she called to ask if I could lend some advice about the funeral arrangements. It was common knowledge among my friends that for years I had been keeping a "Funeral File." This consisted of a collection of announcements, Orders of Service, expenses, to-do lists and, most important, notations on the various readings or eulogies that I found particularly moving or appropriate. Unfortunately my file was growing, but its mere existence made me realize the need for some sort of manual or brochure that would assist people in their time of need.

Research told me that there were hundreds of books on wedding preparation, an event that is usually organized over the course of a year. There were also numerous titles dealing with the various stages of grieving. There was, however, little available on the ins and outs of planning a funeral— an event for which you are rarely emotionally prepared, and one that can be hugely expensive and, in ordinary circumstances, takes place within a few days of the death. In England, there is a committee that meets four times a year. Its job is to review the planning and protocol for the funerals of each member of the Royal Family. (Since Princess Diana had lost her H.R.H. status, she was no longer on the list.) Although most of us are obviously not dealing with events of that magnitude, it gives credence to the need for organization and attention to detail.

While it is important to have a ceremony that pays the utmost respect to the deceased, it is also important to remember that it is the living who attend the service. Ideally, it will be tasteful, inclusive, and appropriate for the immediate family. Sadness, shock, anger and guilt are the most obvious emotional hurdles. While the first thoughts of those who are grieving might tend to avoidance and seclusion, it is necessary to appreciate the importance of working through the initial pain to permit some "closure," both for yourself and for others who are grieving.

This book is intended only as a guide. It will explain some of the procedures required by law. It will make you aware of some of the options available to make the service more personal, and it will list some of the details that you might not think of in your grief. It adheres to the traditions of the Protestant church but also includes some of the more common customs of other religions. It is, at best, a guide. The rules have relaxed, the rights and wrongs of protocol are less defined, and there is much more room for personal expression.

My information is based in Ontario though the procedure is nationwide. For the sake of simplicity, I have used the third person singular, masculine.

PRE-ARRANGEMENT

Most of us have, hidden somewhere, a copy of our last will and testament, stating whom we want as our executor and how we want our property divided. This is the very least that your family would hope to find. To die "intestate" (without a will) pretty well guarantees that the probate will take longer, that it will be more costly, and that things will not necessarily be done the way you might have wished. In a perfect world, you would have everything documented, from the wish to have organs donated, through to a list of various investments and insurance policies, even your wishes regarding your own funeral. Ideally this information is in the hands of your executor or lawyer. If this information is tucked away with your will in a safety deposit box that no one knows about, it may not be discovered until after the funeral, when the will is read.

There is an organization in Ontario, the Funeral Advisory and Memorial Society, that can advise you on how to arrange and pre-pay your own funeral. Also, the Ontario Funeral Service Association has a detailed guide for organizing your affairs. If these details have been taken care of, you are fortunate indeed. Unfortunately, in most families this is not the case and many decisions are thrust upon the survivors.

Remember too that even if you have given the power of attorney to someone, that person has the right to make decisions on your behalf only when you are "incompetent," not when you are dead.

For a list of things that can be arranged in advance, see Appendix A.

THE FIRST STEPS

What Happens to the Body?

If a person dies in hospital or in a nursing home, the attending doctor will sign the death certificate and notify the family and the deceased person's family doctor. If the death is outside a hospital — for example, unexpectedly at home, or in a car accident — the coroner and the police must be called, along with the family doctor. All caution must be taken to not unnecessarily alarm the family. An autopsy (post-mortem) must be performed by a coroner to determine the exact cause of death. In some cases an inquest will be called. This is an official inquiry, usually before a jury, to determine the cause of death.

When a terminally ill patient chooses to go home to die, doctors are encouraged to sign the death certificate without calling a coroner, thus allowing "Death With Dignity." Unfortunately, in some rare situations, there are doctors so afraid of being accused of "assisted suicide" that they request an unnecessary autopsy even when the cause of death is known, creating a huge intrusion on the family.

For the purpose of this book, I am assuming that the family will use a funeral home. A funeral home can offer a wide range of services and generally helps facilitate the process. There are alternatives to a funeral home discussed later in this book.

On notification of a death, the family should contact a funeral home. They are always available, regardless of the hour. They will take charge of transporting the body. If necessary, your doctor or minister can supply you with the name of a reliable home in your area. Other members of the family should be contacted, as well as the deceased's employer, lawyer, minister and executor.

If the death occurred in hospital or a nursing home, the personal effects of the person who died must be removed. If the immediate family chooses not to do this, it is a task easily handed over to a caring friend, or a relative outside the immediate family.

If the death happened away from home, it is often necessary that someone make a positive identification of the body. Again, this does not have to be done by the most grieved person, but often there is a need for the bereaved to see the deceased no matter how traumatic that might be. After the tragic crash of Flight 111, in Peggy's Cove, Nova Scotia, on September 3, 1998, the relatives were devastated at not being able to identify the bodies.

If there is a need to transport the body, arrangements can be made through a reputable funeral home. This home can be in the city where the death occurred or in your hometown. The body must be placed in a flight pack that meets the requirements of the airline. If in a foreign country, embassies and consulates can be helpful. Also most airlines have a "compassionate travel" policy (discussed later, under Funeral Home.)

After the body has been dealt with, close friends should be contacted. They will give you support and help with the inevitable circle of telephone calls. These calls should be delegated and should include distant relatives, business colleagues, church and club associates, and childhood friends. To save a second phone call, tell them in which newspapers the obituary will appear. It is better that someone is called twice than overlooked.

"God grant me the serenity to accept the things I cannot change, the courage to change the things I can, and the wisdom to know the difference."

—Anonymous

MILITARY SERVICE

There is an organization called the Last Post Fund whose mandate is to ensure a dignified burial for all war veterans. A means test is required, and they are careful to state that no decision on eligibility will be made before the funeral. For information on eligibility, the next of kin should call the nearest office; in Ontario it is 416-923-1608.

The funeral home may have a flag to place on the casket.

FAMILY

The Dynamics

It is to be hoped that the family will gather and important decisions can be made without too much controversy. Flexibility and tolerance are essential. Often, past differences will vanish and petty oppositions remain unexpressed. However, there is much written on celebrations and rituals that indicates the opposite. At times like these, family dynamics are at their strongest and play themselves out in full — sibling rivalry and old feelings regarding some perceived favouritism by a parent, for instance. Quite often these issues are resolved but unfortunately they can be exacerbated. The presence of a trusted friend or clergy as a resource person and listener might help alleviate any tensions.

Try to listen to everyone's wishes and take them all into consideration. Emotions are high. Diplomacy reigns. Ultimately it is the person closest to the deceased who should have the last say.

"We understand death for the first time when he puts his hand upon one whom we love."

—Madame de Stael

CHILDREN

How Can You Help Them?

Regardless of who has died, your children will be affected. Try to include them in the plans and decisions as much as is appropriate for their age and attachment to the deceased. Try to be sensitive to their moods and remember they are children. The fact that they want to play baseball is not only normal but probably healthy. We all grieve at different times and in different ways.

When my nephew died at the age of fourteen, my children were six and seven and too young, I thought, to be involved. Years later I learned how confused and isolated they had felt and wish I had included them in the celebration of Chris' life. One cannot underestimate the importance of their inclusion.

FRIENDS

How Can They Help You?

Besides the initial phoning, there are many ways that friends can help. They want to be there for you and it helps their own grieving if they can share some of the responsibility along with some of the pain.

Close friends will probably come to your house immediately, and their assistance can be enormous. They can call friends and family with the funeral plans, answer the door and the telephone, and make lists of callers. They can also keep track of food donations (Cheryl and David Brown — chicken casserole for eight — Pyrex dish to be returned — labelled and put in freezer), list the flowers that have been sent to the house or to the funeral home (family of Sarah and Bill Baxter — large arrangement of pink roses, card attached) and note the donations to charities (Fred and Susan Kelly, Bereaved Families of Ontario).

They may go to the library and search out a particular poem or reading you want to include in the funeral service. Other tasks might include looking after the children, walking the dog or taking the dog to the kennel. They could also help with airport pickups and hotel arrangements for out-of-town guests. They might clean, change beds, prepare meals, or buy stationery or even a special register book. Close relatives of the deceased have a great fear of forgetting both the events surrounding the funeral and the deceased himself. A "Memory Book" could be started by someone close, detailing thoughts and happenings.

Remember that people are there to help you and you will be doing them a favour if you let them. Also remember that this is one time you do not have to have anyone around if you do not want them around. The nosy neighbour or the sometime friend may not have a role in your life right now. If not-so-close friends visit your home, they can be politely turned away at the door. The person designated to answer the door can say you are resting or with your family. It is to be hoped that distant friends will send a note rather than telephone, as the phone will be busy with arrangements for the funeral.

"One does not know, till one is a bit at odds with the world, how much one's friends who believe in one rather generously, mean to one."

—D. H. Lawrence

LEGAL REQUIREMENTS

Necessary Certificates and Documents

The funeral director plays an important role at this stage. He will go to the hospital and pick up the death certificate from the attending physician. He will prepare the "Statement of Death," necessary under the Vital Statistics Act, from information gained from the family or the executor. He will then take the death certificate and the statement of death and register the death with the Registrar General's Office. At this time he will get a burial permit required by law from the Registrar. This permit is valid for interment or cremation.

If the deceased is to be cremated, the next of kin or executor must sign an application for a cremation certificate from the coroner.

MEDICAL DONATIONS

Organs

In 2000, the Ontario Government legislated the Trillium Gift of Life Network Act in order to expedite organ and tissue donation. If the deceased has filled out a donation card or the section so designated on his driver's license, his wishes are legally binding. If no donor card is available then the decision is up to the next of kin. This decision must be made immediately because, for obvious reasons, time is of the essence. A trusted friend or clergy could help mediate with the hospital staff. For organ donation, the body must be artificially oxygenated with a ventilator until the organ can be retrieved. This is not necessary for tissue donation as there is no need for the blood flow to be maintained. For more information, contact 1-800-263-2833 or www.giftoflife.on.ca

It is important to note that the donation of organs is confidential and that it does not affect the decision to have the casket open.

The Canadian National Institute for the Blind in Toronto is partnered with the Eye Bank. If the deceased wants his eyes donated, the attending doctor knows the procedure. Their 24-hour number is 416-480-7465.

Whole Body to Medical Science

The deceased may wish to donate his body to research for the teaching of professionals. For more information contact the medical school of your choice or the Chief Coroner at 1-877-991-9959. The family is required to pay for the transportation of the body to the university. They, in turn, will arrange for the cremation of the body. Not all bodies are accepted, for instance if they have been autopsied or embalmed. If possible, one should make application in advance.

If you have donated your organs, you can not do a "whole body donation."

Medical Aids

Many medical aids can be donated:
- hearing aids to the Canadian Hearing Society
- eyeglasses to Third World countries, through the Lion's Club
- wheelchairs and walkers to nursing homes or hospitals
- pacemakers can sometimes be refurbished through a hospital

The funeral home must be notified about a pacemaker if the body is to be cremated.

"Man is harder than rock and more fragile than an egg."
—Yugoslav Proverb

NOTES

THE FUNERAL HOME

Cautions

It is of utmost importance that you visit the funeral director as soon as possible because so many decisions have to be made. If the deceased has not previously selected a home, be sure to choose one that is reputable. Members of the Ontario Funeral Service Association, for instance, adhere to a strict code of ethics. While most homes are there to help you through a difficult time and do so with great skill and sensitivity, there are always stories of families who feel that they made some wrong decisions. For this reason it is wise not to send the most grieved person to the home alone. Their vulnerability puts them at risk of making unwise decisions. Remember that you are entering into a business agreement and a clear head can help make financially sound decisions while still adhering to the family's wishes. A second or third person can help with the decisions and maintain control over the situation.

Be sure to discuss the costs of various services offered so that you come away with a clear picture of your commitment and theirs. It is also worth noting that funds may not be immediately available, in which case, method of payment becomes a topic. You could need court permission to pay costs. It is also paramount to remember the financial situation of the family. I do not think anyone would want to bankrupt their family on a funeral.

What to Take With You

There are some things you should bring to the funeral home. You will need to take clothes for the deceased. You will also need to bring certain pieces of information regarding the deceased to assist in the legal paperwork. These are date and place of birth; marital status; names, dates of birth and places of birth of deceased's parents; maiden name of the deceased's mother; religious name; Social Insurance Number; birth certificate; citizenship or naturalization papers; military discharge papers.

For a complete list of what to take to the funeral home, see Appendix B.

Services Offered

The funeral director and his staff are there to help you and they offer a wide range of services. Keep in mind, however, that there is a charge for each one.

At your request, they will notify newspapers, arrange for flowers, and provide ushers and limousines.

Much of their advice is free and willingly given, for example, on protocol and procedure, and, if you are from out of town, the name of a minister, organist, florist or caterer.

As you make the arrangements for the funeral, you can decide how much you want to cope with and where you want them to assist. These decisions are often purely financial.

Other things available from funeral homes include a room for visitation complete with attendants, coffee and sandwiches if you wish; a chapel for the service; a selection of caskets and urns from which to choose; offer to deal with any charity selected for donations; provision of stationery including a register book, thank you notes, "In Memoriam" cards; arrangement of payment to the newspapers, the minister, organist, soloist and anyone else deemed necessary.

"The body dies but the spirit is not entombed."
—Buddhism: Dhammapada 151

For a complete list of services offered by the funeral home, see Appendix C.

For a list of potential expenses for a funeral, see Appendix D.

Alternatives To A Funeral Home

There are new discount funeral stores opening. These provide containers, wreaths, stationery — everything one would need for a funeral. It is against Ontario law for a funeral home to require that you buy the casket from them or to refuse you services if you have bought your casket from somewhere else. Because of this, some funeral homes have lowered the price of their caskets but raised the price of their services. Comparative shopping can become very complicated at a time when people are most vulnerable. Remember that if you buy a casket at a discount store, you will have to pay to have it delivered. You will also need insurance and you must have someone there to accept delivery of the body. For sure, the least expensive way to have a funeral is to arrange everything yourself, for example, the casket, transportation, legal documents, burial arrangements. There are also licensed transfer services whose job is to pick up the body, place it in a container and deliver it to a cemetery or crematory. Funeral homes, however, are in business because they can lead you through this process with a minimum of confusion.

Compassionate Travel

It is possible that the body will have to be

transported to another city. Arrangements must be made through the funeral homes at either end. The body travels in a flight pack, which is provided by the funeral home, in the cargo part of the plane.

Most airlines have a policy on compassionate travel for family members. Air Canada, for instance, requires the name, address, and telephone number of the funeral home plus the date of the service. The airline may call the funeral home to verify. A copy of the death certificate is necessary, and the obituary, while not necessary, might help expedite the process. If no information is available, you may be required to purchase the ticket. You will then be reimbursed at a later date after producing your boarding pass and a copy of the death certificate and filling out a bereave travel refund form, available at Air Canada ticket offices. These forms must be submitted within ninety days. The policy is very generous, including common-law, in-law, and same-sex partners. Air Canada gives a reduction of 75 percent of the regular fare.

PREPARATION OF THE BODY

Embalming

The description of the procedure for embalming is unpleasant (for details, see Glossary) and, contrary to popular belief, it is not necessary to embalm the body in Ontario unless it is being transported out of province or on public transport within the province. The body can, in fact, be refrigerated instead. The reason for embalming is simply to avoid the onset of rigor mortis and to make the tissue more pliable for cosmetology, a procedure that is done whether the casket is open or closed.

Cosmetology

This service prepares the body for viewing and involves grooming and the shaping and colouring of the face. A recent picture of the deceased can assist greatly. Very often the decision for the casket to be open or closed is reversed at the last minute.

With many people there is a need to view even a disfigured body in order to help give "closure."

Clothes

You will be asked to bring clothes for the deceased to the funeral home. The body will be dressed and groomed even if the casket is to remain closed. Traditionally, they required "Sunday best" clothes: a jacket and tie for a man, subdued colours in a soft material, preferably with a high neck, for a woman. This, however, is no longer cast in stone and is left up to the family's discretion. Similarly, play clothes were not put on children. Nowadays, parents might feel more comfortable with the more familiar attire. Undergarments will also be needed, but no shoes.

Some religions customarily use shrouds or white linen. Military personnel, police and dignitaries have their own protocols.

Wedding rings may or may not be worn by the deceased. Often people want to save the wedding ring as a keepsake or to pass it on to their offspring. It is not customary to wear any other jewellery.

A friend asked permission to go in and dress her deceased husband. She just felt it was something she had to do. No one else could tie his tie the way he liked it.

Family members may put personal items in the casket with the deceased, such as pictures, cards or stuffed animals. These items may be given to the funeral director or, if the casket is to be open, they may be placed personally before the first visitation. This "participation" is often helpful for children.

Isabella Smedja wrote a beautiful story about her father's death and her gathering of "grave goods" for his casket. She sewed little silk pouches into which she put miniature figurines of things that were important to him; a dog, a horse, a soccer ball. Another pouch held foreign coins from countries he had visited. The third was full of semiprecious stones, one for each of his children and grandchildren.

"Faith is the bird that feels the light when the dawn is still dark."

— Rabindramath Tagone

CHOOSING A CASKET OR URN

Costs

One of the biggest expenses you must be prepared for is the casket. They range greatly in price depending on the type of material, the fittings and the lining. Again, it is important to keep things in perspective. No one is going to judge you on the type of casket you choose, if, in fact, they even notice.

Most funeral homes offer a wide selection from which to choose. These include different types of wood, bronze, copper and steel. For obvious reasons the casket must be strong and, if the body is to be cremated, the casket must be combustible. There are also now specialty retail stores in many large cities, some selling designer caskets. Be aware of added shipping costs. It is now legal to rent a casket, which you might consider if the body is to be cremated. Humphrey Funeral Home in Toronto, for instance, offers a choice of four. The rented casket would be used for the visitation and or service, after which, the body is placed in a simpler container for cremation. The interior is completely replaced after each rental and this procedure could half the cost of the casket.

Considerations

If there is to be a memorial service, the casket is not even present. A friend paid a fortune for his father's casket and the cremation took place two days before the service, with no one present.

Often, the casket is draped with a tapestry of flowers, a flag or a pall. We chose a comfortable oak casket for my father, paying particular attention to the grain of the wood, forgetting the Anglican custom of covering the casket with a pall for the service.

Jewish caskets are constructed out of wood, using wooden pegs. No carving or varnish is allowed.

A concrete vault or outer container, which is air tight and water tight, is sometimes required by cemeteries. It is placed in the grave and the casket is lowered into it. These outer cases are now available from most funeral homes.

Urns

If the body is cremated, the remains will be placed in a plastic container called an urn. More substantial and decorative urns may be purchased from the funeral home. The choice depends on what will ultimately happen to the remains. This can be personalized. For a recent death in our family, my nephew made an urn from a piece of antique pine. We delivered this to the funeral home and they put the ashes in it.

Open or Closed?

This decision is one of the most difficult and, in the Protestant Church, is left up to the family. Because the body is prepared for viewing, the decision can be made at the last minute. Some people prefer to remember the deceased as he was, and others need to see the actual body to help with "closure." This is an individual choice.

Quite often the casket remains open for the family to say goodbye privately and then is closed immediately before the first public visitation. It can also be left open until the service.

The casket is closed for a Protestant service. In some other churches it is left open and the mourners file by to say goodbye, often touching or kissing the deceased. It is important to remember that you are under no obligation to view the body. As a member of the family or as a friend, it is not wrong to bypass the casket and go directly to the immediate family and give your condolences. There are situations, however, where you are physically required to walk past the casket to get to the family. (On rare occasions, part of the body might be draped, in the case of an accident, for instance).

In the Roman Catholic Church, the casket is

closed during Mass. In the Greek Orthodox Church it is open during Mass.

There is never a viewing in an Orthodox Jewish funeral. The casket is always closed. Reform Jews tend to be more flexible and may allow an open casket.

TYPES OF FUNERALS

The funeral selected depends on a number of things. A key factor is the whereabouts of the immediate family. For example, if a son were hitchhiking around Asia, or otherwise out of contact, the family might choose to go ahead with a private burial followed by a memorial service on his return. (Alternatively, it could be done in the reverse order).

Other factors include the religious beliefs of the deceased and his family, the expected size of the funeral, the age of the deceased, and the availability of a facility, location and parking.

A funeral service may be held in a church, a chapel, the chapel of the funeral home, in a private home, at a crematorium, or at the graveside. A thanksgiving service may be held anywhere — in the open air, at sea, in a private home.

Private

This service is held for family and only the closest of friends. Invitation is by a handwritten note or a telephone call. Often it is followed by a memorial service where the public may attend. One should not attend a private service unless invited.

Traditional

At this service, the casket is present, either located at the front or entering as part of the processional. This service is usually held in a church or in the chapel of the funeral home. If burial does not follow the service, there is usually an explanation in the Order of Service, for example "Private burial to take place at a later date."

"Fear not that life will come to an end, but rather fear that it will never have a beginning."
—John Henry Cardinal Newman

Memorial

A memorial service often takes on the air of a celebration. The body is not present and is buried or cremated privately either before or after the service.

This service is also used in the rare situation when there are no remains.

Thanksgiving

This is a more informal service with speeches, readings and eulogies done spontaneously.

Home

Here, the largest room is selected, preferably one that can be closed off from the rest of the house. A little altar can be made, and the casket rests at the front. The funeral home will provide chairs and transportation of the body. The family can sit alone, off to the side. Live music or taped music may be used.

"There is no death, only a change of worlds."
—Chief Seattle of the Dwamish Tribe

THE OBITUARY

An obituary is usually placed in the local newspaper and any other paper that is appropriate, for example, home town, business news, locations of foreign postings. It is important to get the obituary into the chosen newspapers as soon as possible to give friends and family time to make their travel arrangements. This, however, is a service you pay for and it can add up quickly. For example, ten lines for three days in the *Globe & Mail* is over $200, based on a per line (40 letters), per day fee that gets less expensive the more days used. A photograph is $160 per day. Unless organized through the funeral home, you must prepay with a credit card.

If the deceased is a dignitary, the newspaper might choose to write their own article and may have pertinent details on file. If the deceased had been ill for a long time, the outline of his obituary may have been dealt with and you only need to add the funeral and visitation information.

The easiest way to write an obituary is to look at old newspapers and follow a format that is suitable. It can be as long and as detailed as you wish, but remember that the cost can be considerable.

The funeral director can arrange to have your

notice faxed to whichever newspapers you choose. Just be sure you proofread the copy before he sends it; this is not a time for mistakes. The newspaper might call the family to confirm details.

The obituary can appear one day or it can run up to and including the day of the funeral. That is the family's decision.

It should include:

- Last name, first and middle names, including nicknames (Maiden name), place of residence.
- Date of death; may also include "suddenly," or "after a long illness."
- Location: for instance, "at home," "while vacationing in New York."
- It is not necessary to state cause of death but this appears more frequently now: for example, "after a courageous battle with cancer."
- Age did not used to be stated except in the case of a child or to avoid confusion between Senior and Junior; however, it is now commonly mentioned.
- Daughter of_____.
- Spouse of or predeceased by _____.
- Remembered by _____. (Daughters used to be listed before sons but now it is more likely to be chronological). Children's spouses should be mentioned here, often with the use of parenthesis, i.e., son William (Carolyn).
- Living children should be listed before dead.
- It is appropriate to list grandchildren and is often very important for their relationship to be so acknowledged.

- The history can be as detailed as you wish.
- Professional achievements, school or honorary degrees, clubs, directorships, volunteer work, awards, boards, military service.
- Details of funeral arrangements and visitation times.
- Be sure to give address of funeral home and church if you are using both.
- It is now often customary to choose a charity (or more than one) to be the recipient of memorial donations. You might say, for instance, "Donations to Heart and Stroke would be appreciated." The choice of charity is usually related to the deceased's life (the foundation of a university) or to his death (the Heart and Stroke Foundation). You may wish to name the particular local chapter and include addresses of the charities chosen.
- You can also say "to the charity of your choice."
- Be careful with the use of words such as "lovingly" and "beloved" lest they make a mockery of a failed relationship.

"Sorrow is like a precious treasure, shown only to friends."
—African Proverb

Check the newspapers for sample obituaries.

NOTES

VISITATION

Purpose

Visitation allows friends and colleagues to pay their respects to the family and, if the casket is present, to say goodbye to the deceased. It is the family's choice if and when to have it. Most frequently it is the afternoon and evening on the day before the funeral (from 2 to 4 P.M. and 7 to 9 P.M.) This usually allows out-of-town family to be present. The choice is also for the convenience of the visitors. Older people prefer to visit in the afternoon and people with day jobs prefer to not take time off work to pay their respects. It also accommodates people who work shifts (the staff at a nursing home, for instance). People coming from out of town may choose to come to the evening visitation and stay overnight for the funeral. (Do not argue with anyone who insists on staying at a hotel. You will have enough on your mind.)

If the deceased was very old, with few remaining friends, and a small turnout is expected, it is possible to have an hour's visitation just before the funeral.

The body does not have to be present (see types of funerals).

Try to have some family members present at

all times during visitation. The family usually stands near the entrance. It is helpful to have someone who is comfortable with people at the start of the line, as the visitors are often grieved and uncomfortable. Try to introduce family members, particularly children. It expands the circle, but what is more important, it allows visitors to speak to those whom they know, or should know, but may not recognize.

It is likely that friends will want to share stories and remember events that included the deceased. These tales can be both comforting and emotional, and the Kleenex provided by the funeral home will come in handy. Remember it is okay to show your emotions, and your doing so allows others to do the same.

It has become quite common to have large collages and framed photographs of the deceased with his family and friends in the room. The funeral home usually can provide you with an easel for display.

A friend prepared a wonderful "memory table" for his father who was a real character. It included the Santa Claus outfit he entertained children in for forty years, his golf clubs, a number of blown-up newspaper articles, and photos. It put people at ease and brought to memory a number of heart-warming stories.

Coffee and cookies are also usually provided by the funeral home.

Some homes have another room where parents can take children who need to get out of the big room for a while.

Be sure to have security at your home during this time, because visitation hours are made public in the newspaper.

Procedure

Guests are first met by staff from the home who will take their coats. They will be asked to sign a register book, provided by the home or brought in by you. It is helpful if visitors sign their full name for easy identification. It used to be that only one person of a couple would sign, for example, Sarah & Brian, or Mr. and Mrs. B.H. Cowan, however, it is now customary for both partners to sign. Spouses or family members who are not present should not be included. It is confusing for the family members who feel they missed seeing someone.

To facilitate donations to the chosen charity, it is appropriate to have information and envelopes available. These will be provided by the grateful organization.

A tray should be placed for Mass cards.

If the casket is present, guests will go there

first to pay their respects and then come to the family. (It is not uncommon for guests to bypass an open casket.) It is helpful if guests introduce themselves, as the family is dealing with many faces and might even forget the name of a close neighbour.

As a guest, it is important to respect the wishes of the family while adhering to your beliefs. You do not, for instance, have to kneel just because a bench is there. A bowed head and a moment of silence are appropriate.

A divorced spouse or relative may choose to visit the home rather than cause an awkward situation at the funeral. Quite often, if children are involved, it is wise to do what works best for them, which may include sitting with them at the funeral or just sending flowers and a note. It is to be hoped that your instincts and open dialogue will dictate what is best.

"When one is helping another, both are strong."

— German Proverb

NOTES

TRIBUTES

Flowers

The family of the deceased may choose to encourage charitable memorial donations instead of flowers. In this case, it is customary for family and close friends only to send flowers. The florist will be able to advise you, for example, children usually choose to send a casket spray.

You usually send flowers "In Memory Of" or "To The Funeral Of." Put your full name for easy recognition, recording and acknowledgment. It used to be that the flowers were sent to the lady of the house or to the nearest relative, and that the death was never mentioned, but instead, "Thinking of you." It is now appropriate to send them to whomever you are closest to and to say you were sorry to hear about the death of_____. If you did not know the deceased, send them to the home of the person you do know. Some flowers may be selected to go with the casket to the cemetery. Others may be distributed among the family or to hospitals or nursing homes. You may want to leave some flowers in the church for the Sunday Service.

Remember, it is never too late to send flowers. It is often thoughtful to send them to the house a week or so after the funeral to show you are still thinking of the bereaved. Marking an anniversary of the death also shows you care and remember.

Never send flowers to Orthodox Jews; however it is becoming more acceptable to send them to Reform Jews. One should check before sending.

Never send flowers to Chinese after the funeral, as they consider them an object of death at a funeral, something that should never be placed among the living.

Charitable Donations

If you decide to have a memorial donation, try to choose a charity with meaning to the deceased. The idea may spring from his volunteer work, an academic association, or the cause of his death.

Be sure to notify the chosen charity and give them the full address of the person to be contacted. The charity should ensure that cards and envelopes are available both at the funeral home and at the church. This is quite appropriate, even helpful. The chosen charity should keep a list of donors that it will send to you. The list will not include specific amounts. It is wise to keep your own list, from the cards you will receive, to avoid any omissions.

It is customary for friends to donate the amount they would have spent on flowers, perhaps even more, as they will receive a tax receipt. For this reason, donors should include a complete mailing address.

Never send money to the home. A club, however, may collect money to offset the cost of a funeral for someone in need. Be very certain that this is appropriate and appreciated.

Memorials

Sometimes a memorial fund is set up into which people can contribute. This is often done in the death of a child or of someone of great import. Its purpose is perpetuity.

In memory of my nephew, a tree was planted at his school and a scholarship in English was set up in his name. Bursaries, the purchase of hospital equipment, a new gymnasium or computer laboratory — the scope of tributes is endless.

"The great use of life is to spend it for something that outlasts it."

—William James

Mass Cards

Often Mass cards are available at the church. These are blank donation cards. You put your full name and address and the amount of your donation. A Mass or service will be performed for the soul of the deceased.

"No person has ever been honoured for what he received. Honour has been the reward for what he gave."

—Calvin Coolidge

THE SERVICE

Usual Format

You and your Minister will be able to work out the details of the Order of Service. It is important that you are comfortable with the format, keeping in mind that in some churches there are rituals and religious practices that must be included.

The service is the same if the body is going to be interred or cremated.

See Appendix E for Order of Service samples.

Readings

Usually there is a reading from both the Old and the New Testament. If there is to be a Communion, a passage from the Gospel always concludes the Readings. The family may choose a member or close friend of the deceased to read. Readings may include more nonconventional authors, for example, Kahlil Gibran or W.H. Auden. (You may ask a friend to find the words in the library or on the internet).

See Appendix F for examples of Biblical and contemporary readings.

To make it easier for your readers, have copies of the readings printed in a decent-size type and double-spaced. The minister will instruct them on how to present the reading, for example, "The first reading...." and how to close, "The word of the Lord." They should confirm with the minister which podium they are going to use. It is helpful if they can practise in location before the service. It is important to note that the language in the service can now be gender inclusive with the use of a new gender-inclusive Bible.

The choice of whether or not Communion is included is not always yours. It depends on the beliefs of the deceased and the church you have chosen. Similarly, certain prayers are always said by the minister including "Prayers of Thanksgiving" and "Rite of Burial."

Hymns are a wonderful addition to a service, and generally you are no longer restricted to traditional choices such as "Abide with me." (See Music, below.)

While the minister usually talks about the deceased's history, it is common to have someone give a eulogy dealing with the more personal side. If the minister is not familiar with the deceased, he may leave that up to the eulogist or he may want to know details, stories, family members' names, memories. Make sure he has the correct information.

Before the service, if they feel up to it, family members are free to mingle with and greet the guests. There is usually a room to the side of the church or chapel where the family may choose to congregate. Close friends or people from out of town who were not able to make visitation may come and pay their respects. At my mother's funeral, just before the procession, the minister had us join hands as he said a final prayer. It was very personal and moving.

Seating

It is best if the seating is arranged so the most grieved have support on either side. This is a time to consider the needs of children. It also helps if those speaking have easy access to an aisle.

If the casket is in place at the front of the church and there is to be no procession, the pall bearers enter and sit in the reserved pews on the left. The family members then enter from the vestry, and take up their places on the right. This can be reversed if the vestry or waiting room is situated on the left. The seating plan should be organized in advance to avoid confusion and to ensure adequate moral support for those in need.

Be prepared for an unexpected relative to arrive. It is also appropriate to save pews for close friends. Just make certain they know, as they would be unlikely to come forward otherwise. If it is a large funeral, empty seats in the reserved pews will be filled just before the start of the service, rather than have people stand.

It is customary for divorced spouses to sit further back unless there is a need for shared children to have their support. Use your common sense, and make the children's emotional welfare your number-one priority.

Recording

A number of churches have a sophisticated sound system for taping the services for "shut-ins," so it may be possible to tape the whole service. Often, the most grieved barely remember the service, so such a recording could be treasured later. Sometimes the minister offers a copy of his homily for a keepsake. Feel free to ask if this is overlooked.

The funeral director will have brought the guest register from the funeral home to the church where people will be invited to sign. The same rules apply as at the home.

As with the visitation, be sure to have security at your house during the hours of the service. Unfortunately, the service provides an opportunity for robbery.

The Eulogy

In choosing someone to give the eulogy, consider not only his relationship with the deceased but also his ability to speak in public. You want him to feel comfortable and to do justice to the deceased.

It is an honour to be asked to give the eulogy and one that is generally not refused. If, however, you are too emotional or too nervous, you should explain this to the family. The eulogy is meant to be a very touching and personal part of the service, with the attention focused on the deceased—not on the speaker. The contents can be humorous and serious, but no speaker should bring up things unpleasant or unresolved. It is meant to honour, not to demean. There can be more than one speaker. Someone may want to share memories. Someone else may have a poem or a poignant passage to share. It is wise to discuss what each person is going to do so as not to be too repetitious. As with the readers, the eulogist should know which podium he is going to use.

The bravest eulogy I ever heard was by a mother for her daughter. She had no history of public speaking, in fact, she admitted being terrified, and yet it was something she knew she had to do.

Children can add tremendously in this area, but never force or coerce a child, or anyone for that matter, into doing it. My daughter, who was sixteen at the time, gave a lovely eulogy for my mother. It was touching to see Grandma from the eyes of her granddaughter. If possible, I would let a child use his words, not an edited copy. If they want to do it, they will not fail you — and if it is not perfect, who cares?

My brother wrote the eulogy for our father, but was too emotional to read it. The honour was passed to his daughter. It was a touching combination.

I once witnessed a father-son combination. The father was the best friend of the deceased and the son was his godchild. They took turns reading the text they had prepared together, knowing that at any moment one could have taken over for the other. It worked beautifully.

Some ministers do not wish the personal eulogy to usurp the religious element of the service and will typically look for a careful balance between the personal remembrances and the religious teachings. In some churches, for example, recently, in certain Roman Catholic dioceses, personal eulogies are not permitted.

"All sorrows can be born if you put them into a story or tell a story about them."

– Isak Dinesen

Music

It used to be that meaningful and traditional hymns were interspersed into the service. Things have become much less restricted and much more informal. The music is more likely to reflect the tastes and life of the deceased than the teachings of Christ. And it works. Within limits, this is an opportunity to really personalize the service.

My first experience was with the untimely and sudden death of a twenty-year-old girl. As we entered the church, we were accompanied by a medley of her favourite CDs and tapes, lovingly prepared by her brother. Not only did it emphasize the tragedy of losing one so young, it was a chance for the brother to really participate in his sister's funeral. It was also, I imagine, a conduit for his grief.

An organ is helpful to carry the tune and the voices, but I have also been at services with a piano and a guitar. Choirs, when they can be arranged, add beautiful harmony; however, you will be restricted to choosing what they are familiar and comfortable with. A soloist allows a contemplative reprieve.

I have been present for both a piper and a bugler, both of which were lovely.

A school song may be sung, particularly if the school has been part of a family tradition. Similarly, a camp song may be appropriate.

The music may also be seasonal, something that works beautifully at Christmas.

In a recent article in the New York *Times,* Sarah Lyall discusses the trend towards less traditional selections, as evidenced in Elton John's moving rendition of "Candle in the Wind" at the funeral for Diana, Princess of Wales. In the article, Ben Jason of Co-operative Funeral Services in Britain says, "There are three kinds of reasons that people choose specific music. One is to set the scene, usually with somber and reflective music. Two, it is reflective of the individual concerned. The third reason is that it was selected by the deceased, or was his or her favourite song."

For some traditional ideas and for the most popular modern selections, see Appendix G

Pall Bearers

The pall bearers attend the casket at a funeral. It is best if they can be asked in person, and, as it is an honour to be asked, one that is usually not refused unless one is ill or away. Pall bearers may now be selected from women and from the immediate family, which is a break from tradition. My parents were honoured with their grandchildren. The two who were absent were listed on the Order of Service as "And With Us From Afar."

Pall bearers are not necessary at a memorial service or any service where the casket is not present.

It is mostly an honorary duty, as the caskets are placed on wheels and generally transported, using the handles on the side, by the funeral home staff. It may be necessary to lift the casket into the hearse or to the graveside. In which case, it is prudent to have the stronger pall bearers at the corners, as the casket alone could weigh fifty pounds.

In North America, the casket is only carried shoulder high in the case of state or military funerals. It is not wrong to do it, but it is very physically demanding. The pall bearers in this case are chosen because they are strong and of equal height rather than for their closeness to the deceased.

The number of pall bearers is no longer restricted but is usually six. Any number of honorary pall bearers and flower bearers is accepted.

Honorary pall bearers walk two by two in front of the casket. (See Procession, below). It is no longer obligatory for them to wear black.

Ushers

Along with pall bearers, ushers are chosen to escort the guests to their pews. It is best to select friends who are likely to know who is who and therefore know where to seat them. Close friends should be escorted to the front, acquaintances in the middle. Late arrivals come up the side aisle.

The ushers stay at the back of the church if there are pall bearers. If there are no pall bearers, and there is a procession, they walk in front of the casket. In either case, one or two ushers should remain at the back in case of late arrivals.

If necessary, the funeral home or the sexton of a large church can provide ushers. It is now acceptable to use women and children. Ushers, like pall bearers, are no longer obliged to wear black.

Procession

It is customary for the casket to be placed on a church "truck" with wheels before the service starts. The members of the procession assemble and usually enter from the rear of the church. The minister or priest leads the procession, followed by the altar boys (if a Catholic Mass) and anyone else who is serving, including the choir. Next come the pall bearers, two by two, in front of the casket. Next is the chief mourner. Strictly speaking the order is by age and relation to the deceased, but it is more important to ensure that everyone has needed support. Two nieces may be best friends and would be best going together. A stronger child may well offer better support than an older sibling. As the family is being seated, the funeral home officials place the casket on a stand and then quietly move out of sight.

If there is to be no procession, the casket is placed on the stand at the front of the church before the service. The family enters from the door nearest their pews. Depending on the size and layout of the church, the casket can be opened and made available for mourners to pay their respects up to an hour before the funeral begins. The casket is closed before the service and remains closed thereafter.

Recession

The order of the Recession is the same as in the procession except that the choir remains at the front of the church. When there is no casket, the family may return to the vestry to collect themselves or may leave down the centre aisle. This latter option allows them a chance to visit with anyone who might not go to the wake. Staff from the funeral home are excellent at advising you and your guests on procedures.

At the funeral of a dear friend's father, the minister led the recession holding a picture of the deceased on the forehead of his bowed head as he retreated. It was an effective way to allow everyone to say goodbye.

Limousines

It is not necessary to have limousines to transport the family but it does eliminate any bereaved person from having to drive and it does look uniform. It also allows needed privacy. It is, of course, an added cost.

Most cities have companies that provide this service. The funeral home also may have cars available. Some people prefer to use dark-coloured cars driven by friends.

Cars may be provided for just the immediate family, or the number may be expanded to include readers, pall bearers, ushers, spouses of pall bearers.

The distances between venues may affect your decision.

Order of Service Bulletin

The Order of Service is a printed guideline of the procedure of the service. It is not necessary; however, its attention to detail can make a funeral run smoothly, without confusion or embarrassment. Visitors from other congregations and religions will feel more comfortable if they know when to stand, when to sit, which book to use, and which page number. It can include the words to creeds and prayers that others know by heart, and words to songs that are not in the Hymnary. The names of the honorary pall bearers, pall bearers and flower bearers are usually listed on the first page after that of the minister and organist. Depending on the time available, the Order of Service can be printed by the church secretary or sent to a printer. It is often done on the regular church bulletin but you can design your own. If, by the time you go to print, you have chosen the readings but are uncertain about the readers, you can say "A member of the family" or omit any reference as to who will participate. This allows some choice for family members who have not yet arrived. It also takes the pressure off a child, or any one for that matter, who is not certain he can do it. Be sure to have enough copies made and remember to have them placed on the front pews for the family and pall bearers.

It is thoughtful to include a line at the bottom to explain what will happen to the body. "Burial to take place immediately after the service at Mount Pleasant Cemetery," or "Private Cremation to take place at a later date." People should be invited to join you at the wake. (See Wake)

A map should be included where needed.

There is much freedom here to personalize. A friend included a short eulogy to his father on the back page that was both touching and memorable. The front page could be a picture of the deceased. An insert can be added with information about the deceased's life. A blank sheet of paper may be included with an invitation to guests to jot down any memories they have of the deceased and to drop them in a "Memory Box" at the back of the church. This is a wonderful keepsake for the family.

In addition to the bulletin, memorial cards are often provided by the funeral home. Typically, these are small folded cards featuring the deceased's name and dates, perhaps a reading, psalm, picture or personal remembrance.

"Some memories are realities and are better than anything that can ever happen to one again."

—Willa Cather

For example of bulletins, see Appendix E.

NOTES

THE BODY AFTER THE FUNERAL

"No one knows the story of tomorrow's dawn."

—African Proverb

Cremation

It is becoming more common for the body to be cremated. This decision does not necessarily affect the type of service you choose. Committal prayers, which are a necessary part of a funeral, can be said at the appropriate time, either at the church, at the crematorium, or at the grave.

The casket is taken to a crematorium where it is placed in a ceramic "retort" and subjected to intense heat. This is organized by the funeral director. It takes approximately two or three hours to reduce the remains to ashes; however, the whole process takes a few days.

The remains are than put into a previously chosen plastic, wood, stone, ceramic or metal urn or one provided by the family.

There are a number of choices on what to do with cremated remains. The urn may be buried in a family plot in a cemetery, or in an urn garden. Another option is "inurnment" in a niche in a "columbarium." The niche is designed to hold an urn. It is recessed and the front may be either glass or a nontransparent material such as granite or bronze. A series of niches is called a columbarium and is constructed out of a variety of materials from cement to bronze. Columbaria can be part of an interior structure or part of an outdoor setting such as a garden.

An urn may also be buried in an unmarked common grave with no marker to identify its whereabouts. The crematorium, however, does record the location.

The urn may not be buried on your property; however, it may be kept in one's home.

Scattering of the ashes over land or water is legal in most areas. Scattering gardens are also available in most cemeteries. A friend requested his ashes be scattered over the lake where he had spent many a happy summer.

It is important to note that the ashes are, in fact, bone fragments, with a weight of up to nine pounds. This procedure can be quite traumatic for those involved if they are not prepared.

Interment of Non-cremated Remains

This usually takes place immediately following the service. The casket and chosen flowers are placed in the hearse, often followed by an extra car for flowers. (This car may take a faster route to the cemetery to ensure the flowers are in place when the procession arrives.) The pall bearers go in front of the hearse, the family follows the hearse. Guests fill in behind.

Usually a small flag or "Funeral" sign is placed on the hood of each car to identify it as a member of the cortege. It is important to try to keep together, especially for out-of-town people who may not know the location of the cemetery.

The use of headlights is no longer effective, but blinkers may be used. Police escorts are often present to stop traffic at lights, but this service must be arranged in advance and is an additional expense. It is not legal to go through a red light unless a policeman is present. You can also arrange to have parking restrictions removed in the area of the church.

It used to be that traffic pulled off to the side of the road to allow the procession to pass. This show of respect is quite difficult on busy city streets and is more likely found only in smaller towns.

At the grave, people are asked to gather around for the prayers of committal. The casket may then be lowered into the grave, though some may choose to have this done later by the cemetery staff.

Sometimes flowers are passed out to be placed on the casket, or a shovel might be passed from person to person, each of whom takes a turn throwing dirt on the grave.

Burial is delayed if, for instance, the cemetery is too far away or the ground is frozen and inaccessible.

The casket could also be placed in a crypt in a mausoleum.

Choosing a Plot

Before you start looking for a suitable plot, be certain that there is no family plot or that the deceased has not bought one. There should be a deed if he has.

If one must be bought, remember that this is another business transaction. Some cemeteries operate as a public service, on a nonprofit basis. Catholic Cemeteries, in Toronto, for example, are owned by the Toronto Catholic Cemetery Association and are nonprofit.

You may need to think about who else, eventually, will rest with the deceased, and therefore check restrictions regarding number of bodies that can be buried. You may also want to confirm the use of markers and headstones.

Maintenance programs may be bought to ensure the site is well kept. It is possible to buy a plot in a common grave. No marker or headstone is allowed but a record is kept in the cemetery. There is also a section in some cemeteries for children. Some young parents haven't ever imagined they would have to buy a plot, or perhaps they want their child with other children, or they don't have the money or the wish to buy a big plot.

Gravestones

A marker will be placed by the cemetery until you decide what you want to do. This is one of the few decisions you can take your time over, so do. There might be restrictions regarding size and material placed by the cemetery.

Pay attention to any wording of the inscription, as it will be there in perpetuity. You might not want to offend a second wife by having "The One True Love of" on the headstone of the first.

My nephew's grave is marked by a beautiful, huge Georgian Bay rock taken from a place he adored. My parents' stone has an etching of the summer home they created and shared.

"God gave burdens, also shoulders."

—Yiddish Proverb

THE WAKE

It is usual for families to provide an opportunity for mourners and friends to share condolences. Often guests are invited to join the family in the church either immediately following the service or after the interment.

It is customary to serve sandwiches, squares, coffee, tea and cold drinks. These may be prepared by the "Friends of the Church," by friends of the deceased, or by a catering company. Most churches have a committee to deal with setting-up arrangements. Sometimes, there is a nominal charge for the refreshments prepared by this committee.

A friend's dying wish to have wine at his wake, which was to be held in the church, was upheld when the minister himself went and applied for a liquor license.

Depending on the size of the funeral and the proximity of a convenient home, friends might be invited back to a house for the wake. Friends or a caterer may provide the food and assist in setting up everything. It is not inappropriate to have a bar. Remember to include your children's friends. It is important that everyone has support. You may want to invite the minister and even the organist or soloist back to the house.

Not all guests approve of wakes. If a guest feels that way, it is acceptable for him to just drop by briefly to give his condolences. In either case, you might want to consider having family and close friends back to the house. The time together is important, as there can be a terrible denouement after the day's events.

The funeral director usually comes by with the death certificate, the leftover Orders of Service, memorial cards and those from flowers and printed thank-you cards.

A couple of casseroles in the oven will spare you decisions on what to do for dinner. This is one time where you should make full use of your friends' offers of assistance.

"Well everyone can master grief but he that has it."
— William Shakespeare

For a list of things to remember for the wake, see Appendix H.

THANK YOU'S AND ACKNOWLEDGMENTS

"Who does not thank for a little, will not thank for much."

—Estonian Proverb

Thank-you notes are a must, though some families aren't doing them anymore. This chore can easily be divided among family members; however make sure you have a "control" person to double-check. It is better that two notes are sent rather than none. As previously suggested, some friend will have recorded all the donations of flowers, food, special help or thoughtfulness. The funeral home will give you the Mass cards and the donation cards from the donors. Charities will send you a list of those who donated and the total amount to date (without mentioning specific amounts). It is a good idea to cross-reference these with the cards you have. It is important that no one be forgotten. Charities will send their own thank you and a tax receipt, but it is a good idea for you to also acknowledge the gift.

A personal note may be written or you may send a "store-bought" card or (if numbers warrant) a printed card "From the Family of_____." In either case, a personal line should be added along with your signature. Otherwise, do not bother.

The cards supplied by the funeral home tend to be a bit impersonal but are better than nothing and are already covered in your expenses. If someone is unable to send out cards, the task may be delegated. "Mother has asked me....," or "On behalf of all the family...." It is usual for the eulogist, pall bearers, readers, minister, organist and soloist to receive a personal note. It is not necessary to respond to cards unless they included a personal note, but you may choose to do so. It is thoughtful to acknowledge anyone who came to the funeral home when no member of the family was present.

Often, in rural areas, a "thank you" will be placed in the local newspaper. Mention may be made of a special kindness.

If you are having cards printed, you might want to consider a relevant quotation or poem. The most unforgettable card I ever received was from a friend whose drug-addicted, teenage son had committed suicide. It was a picture of him sitting alone on the beach, waves pounding over his feet and it read "Free At Last."

ONE WEEK LATER

I would not pretend to have a solution to the pain of mourning. Your religious beliefs and your heart will dictate when you are ready to move forward. Grieving is a natural process and you must do it at your own speed.

It is a time for friends so, if you can, let them in—but be selective. It is also an extremely difficult time for children, whose level of comprehension often leads to confusion and unanswered questions. Do not neglect them. Their needs are great but they often do not know how to articulate them. They require special attention.

There are hundreds of books available to help you deal with your emotions and those of your family.

There are many organizations that deal with loss and grieving, among them, Bereaved Families and Parents without Partners.

Consult your doctor, hospital, funeral director, clergy or family services to learn what is available in your area. Many organizations offer both group and individual counselling. There are also private practitioners.

"The healthy and strong individual is the one who asks for help when he needs it, whether he's got an abscess on his knee or in his soul."

—Rona Barrett

DIVIDING THE CHATTELS

Unfortunately, while you are trying to put your life back together, there are a number of physical things you may have to deal with. One of the most difficult things to do is divide the family's cherished chattels. No matter how close a family you have, every emotion comes into play and family dynamics might cause tensions. The simple fact that the chattels must be dealt with means there has been a death, and most likely you are all grieving, yet very often there is a need to make decisions quickly.

Sometimes the deceased will have left written instructions as to his wishes; however, these are not binding unless they are part of the will. Also, situations in the family may have changed since these wishes were written. It is a time for tolerance and flexibility.

When my siblings and I were in that situation, we decided on an auction, an equitable method of division of property that my father had demonstrated to us many years before his death. The initial organization was more than we had anticipated, but it all worked beautifully. It was equitable, it was fair and, most important, it was a lot of fun.

"It is easier to rule a kingdom, than to regulate a family."

— Japanese Proverb

If there is not a lot of property and/or inheritors, the decisions are usually easier, however, if there is a large estate, here is a suggestion. List all the major possessions — jewellery, silver, art and furniture. Have these items appraised by professionals — a job that can be divided. Send copies of the appraisals to each inheritor.

Divide the rest of the items into "lots". Do one room at a time. The value of the "lots" will vary because in the same room you might have small pieces of furniture and silver as well as a box of board games. Number each lot and include a list of its contents. Send copies of the listed lots to those involved.

Allow time for each person to inspect the items before the actual auction begins. They can make note of things that interest them. Assemble only the "players" and hold an auction of all the appraised items starting with the most valuable. The only difference is that no money need change hands. For simplicity's sake, imagine that the appraised value was $200,000 and that there were four "players". As long as you spend only your share, in this case $50,000, you never have to pay real money. It is therefore necessary to always know one's own total and the group's total. If the first item goes for $11,000, then the other players know they can spend an equal amount on future items. Let's say at the end of the bidding on the jewellery the totals were

A.	$21,000
B.	$ 9,000
C.	$ 6,000
D.	$ 4,000
TOTAL	$40,000

If the event was to end here, A, who had spent more than his quarter of $10,000, would have owed $11,000 (1 to B, 4 to C and 6 to D). But the bidding continued with the Art, Silver and Furniture. At the end of this part the totals were:

B.	$ 75,000
A.	$ 47,000
C.	$ 42,000
D.	$ 36,000
TOTAL	$200,000

Therefore, B would end up with the most items but he would have to pay cash from his own pocket ($3,000 to A, $8,000 to C, $14,000 to D). At any time, B could have backed off the bidding and kept his total under the estimated $50,000.

When we had our auction, it was actually

fun. There were emotional times but there was no arguing because it was each person's option to bid as high as he wanted. Ridiculous prices—both high and low — were paid. There was much teasing and joking, but we got the job done and I know our parents would have been proud. I also know they would have been sorry to have missed such a day of camaraderie.

The second part deals with the numbered "lots." As you are dealing with one room at a time, the value of the individual "lots" will vary considerably from an armchair down to a box of unknowns marked "goodies." Each person is given a list of the numbered lots and a package of coloured stickers—a different colour for each person.

Using matchsticks or straws, numbers are drawn for the selection process that, in this case would go 1.2.3.4.4.3.2.1.1.2.3.4., etc. The rules are simple:

1. The order must remain the same. (It helps if you have someone keeping track and recording.)

2. You may not move to another room until everything from the previous room has been selected.

3. When you make a choice, you put one of your coloured stickers on it to save any confusion at the end of the day.

Final rule: Each person had to remove his allotment within the next ten days.

CONCLUSION

In spite of the inevitability of death, we are seldom mentally, physically or emotionally prepared for it. You can never fully anticipate your reaction or those of the people closest to you. All of a sudden you are faced with a rush of emotional hurdles, along with a myriad of important decisions, concerns for various family members, the need to fulfill certain legal requirements and, sometimes, unwanted attention.

This book is meant to help prepare you for a funeral, and help you prepare a funeral. It will give you some idea of what you can expect and what is expected of you. You may need the information right now or you may be anticipating some future need. Perhaps you want to know how you can help a friend.

The hope is that this book will guide you through those difficult first days and provide some understanding of the ins and outs of the funeral process. It emphasizes the importance of family and friends, and suggests ways for them to help you. It offers information on common customs and procedures, but above all, it demonstrates how you can make your own personal choices.

In the end, you can share in a service that is memorable and fitting for both the family and the deceased — a celebration of life offering hope for those who are left to grieve. In the words of Kahlil Gibran, "When you are sorrowful look again in your heart, and you shall see that in truth you are weeping for that which has been your delight."

GLOSSARY

AIR TRAY / AIR PACK: A shipping container for a casket. It must meet airline standards.

AUTOPSY: An examination and dissection of a dead body in order to discover the cause of death.

BURIAL: Placing the contained remains in the ground or releasing them at sea.

COFFIN: A European expression for casket.

CLOSURE: A finishing: an end.

CASKET: A case or box to put a dead person into for burial or cremation.

CASKET SPRAY: A blanket of greenery and flowers that covers part or all of the closed casket.

COLUMBARIUM: A structure in a cemetery that contains niches for urns.

COMMITTAL SERVICE: The final ceremony before interment or cremation.

CORONER / MEDICAL EXAMINER: A physician who performs an autopsy to determine the cause of death. He may be asked to investigate further.

CORTEGE: A number of followers or attendants. A ceremonial procession.

COSMETOLOGY: Preparing the body for viewing with the help of a cosmetician and a hairdresser.

CREMAINS: Cremated remains or ashes.

CREMATION: Disposition of the dead body by burning to ashes at a very high temperature.

CREMATORIUM/CREMATORY: A furnace for cremating dead bodies; a building with such a furnace in it.

CRYPT: A chamber or vault serving as a burial place for casketed remains. It can be in a mausoleum or under the main floor of a church.

EMBALM: To keep a dead body from decaying by treating it with various chemicals, usually after removing the viscera, etc.

ENTOMBMENT: The placing of the casketed body in an above ground crypt in a mausoleum.

EULOGY: A speech or writing in praise of a person, event or thing; especially, a formal speech or statement praising a dead person.

GENDER INCLUSIVE: To include both sexes equally.

FUNERAL DIRECTOR: A licensed professional who takes care of the body and helps with the funeral arrangements.

FUNERAL HOME: An establishment in which the dead are prepared for burial or cremation and in which wakes and funerals may be held.

INQUEST: A judicial inquiry into the circumstances surrounding a death.

INTER: To put a dead body into the ground or a tomb; to bury.

INTESTATE: Having made no will; not disposed of by a will.

INURN: To put the ashes of the dead into an urn; to bury; entomb.

LIVING WILL: A document stating one's wishes with regard to life saving procedures. It must be signed, dated and witnessed.

MAUSOLEUM: A large imposing tomb containing crypts for caskets.

NICHE: A compartment in a columbarium for an urn.

OBITUARY / DEATH NOTICE: A notice of someone's death, as in a newspaper, usually with a short biography of the deceased.

PALL: A black, purple or white piece of velvet or other cloth, used to cover a casket, hearse, or tomb; a rich cloth or coverlet.

PALL BEARER: A person who attends or carries the casket at a funeral.

POST-MORTEM: Refers to something done or made after death; post-mortem examination.

POWER OF ATTORNEY: Legal ability or authority; a document giving it.

URN: A vase in any of various forms or materials, usually with a foot or pedestal; such a vase as used to hold the ashes of the dead after cremation.

VAULT: The outer container that a casket is placed into. May be made of a nonpermeable substance.

VISCERA: The inner parts of the body; the internal organs of the body, especially of the thorax and abdomen, as the heart, lungs, liver, kidney, intestines, etc.

WILL: The legal statement of a person's wishes concerning the disposal of his property after death; the document containing this.

APPENDIX A

Things You Can Pre-arrange

Be sure someone responsible knows the whereabouts of information pertaining to the following:

- will, executor, guardian for minor children, division of property
- vital statistics required by funeral home for certificates and registrations, including: name, marital status, date of birth, full names of parents and their dates and places of birth, mother's maiden name, birth certificate (citizenship or naturalization papers), social insurance number, military service discharge, religious name
- funeral arrangements: funeral home, minister, church, cremation or interment, type of casket and/or urn, eulogist, music, pall bearers, ushers, obituary
- place of interment, headstone, inscription
- organ donation and application for donation of body to medical science
- list of contact people: lawyer, minister, doctor, funeral director, investment dealer, banker, insurance agent

List and location of:

- insurance policies (health, life, property, car)
- bank accounts (name of bank, type of account, account number, cancelled cheques)
- mortgages, loans, RRSPs
- location of safety deposit box and key
- pensions (government, employee, disability)
- property deeds, lease information (car, cell phone, etc.)
- income tax information
- licences (marriage, driver)
- credit cards
- military service (branch, awards, service number, rank, date of discharge)
- names and numbers of family and friends
- club memberships

APPENDIX B
What To Take To The Funeral Home

· vital statistics of the deceased (see Appendix A)
· clothes for the deceased, including undergarments (but shoes are not necessary)
· eyeglasses
· a current picture of the deceased for the cosmetologist
· a list of questions
· the obituary (as much of it as you have already composed) and the names of the newspapers you want included

APPENDIX C

Funeral Home Services Typically Offered

- initial interview and assistance with arrangements
- obtaining, preparation and registration of all required documents
- transportation and retaining of the body
- embalming, grooming and cosmetology
- assistance in composing obituary and notification to newspapers
- a selection of caskets and urns from which to choose
- use of visitation facility
- use of chapel for service
- use of premises for reception following the service
- transportation of body to cemetery or crematorium
- hearse, flower car, limousines
- minister, organist, ushers, flowers, caterers
- register, in memoriam cards, thank-you cards
- payment of honorarium to clergy, organist, etc.

APPENDIX D
Potential Expenses Of A Funeral

Be sure to have the details of the estimate in writing.

- funeral home services
- casket
- urn
- outer casket
- coroner's fee
- interment / cremation fee
- opening and closing of grave
- cemetery property
- headstone
- use of funeral home (visitation/service)
- newspapers
- flowers
- phone calls
- hotel, air fare for family
- limousines, flower car
- clergy, organist, soloist
- reception /wake
- stationery
- lawyer and accountant

Sample Order Of Service

A Celebration of the Life of

Margaret Jarvis

December 31, 1943 - November 5, 2002

*A teacher affects eternity; she can never
tell where her influence stops.*

Henry Brooks Adams

Friday, November 8, 2002
3pm

Timothy Eaton Memorial Church
230 St. Clair Avenue West, Toronto, Ontario

Order of Service

ORGAN PRELUDE

CALL TO WORSHIP

OPENING HYMN
No. 240 "Praise My Soul The God Of Heaven"
Lauda Anima

Praise, my soul, the God of heaven;
glad of heart your carols raise;
ransomed, healed, restored, forgiven,
who like me should sing God's praise.
Hallelujah! Hallelujah!
Praise the Maker all your days!

Praise God for the grace and favour
shown our forebears in distress;
God is still the same forever,
slow to chide and swift to bless.
Hallelujah! Hallelujah!
Sing our Maker's faithfulness.

Like a loving parent caring,
God well knows our feeble frame;
Gladly all our burdens bearing,
still to countless years the same.
Hallelujah! Hallelujah!
All within me, praise God's name!

Frail as summer's flower we flourish;
blows the wind and it is gone;
but, while mortals rise and perish,
God endures unchanging on.
Hallelujah! Hallelujah!
Praise the high eternal one.

Angels, teach us adoration,
you behold God face to face;
sun and moon and all creation,
dwellers all in time and space.
Hallelujah! Hallelujah!
Praise with us the God of grace.

PRAYER OF APPROACH

THE LORD'S PRAYER
(in unison)

PSALM READINGS

Psalm 16   *Katherine Sykes*

Psalm 121   *The Rev. Dr. Andrew Stirling*

READINGS FROM CAMP

Jennifer Jarvis

Jenny Wood

SCRIPTURE READING

Romans 12:9-18   *The Rev. Dr. Andrew Stirling*

PERSONAL REMARKS

Charlotte Carter

SOLO

"Teach Your Children"   *Graham Nash*
Pat Cook, Guitar

MEDITATION

The Rev. Dr. Andrew Stirling

PRAYER OF COMFORT

HYMN

No. 232 "Joyful, Joyful We Adore You" *Hymn to Joy*

Joyful, joyful we adore you, God of glory, life and love;
hearts unfold like flowers before you, opening to the sun above.
Melt the clouds of sin and sadness, drive the gloom of doubt away;
giver of immortal gladness, fill us with the light of day.

All your works with joy surround you, earth and heaven reflect your rays,
stars and angels sing around you, centre of unbroken praise.
Field and forest, vale and mountain, flowery meadow, flashing sea,
chanting bird and flowing fountain, sound their praise eternally.

You are giving and forgiving, ever blessing, ever blest,
wellspring of the joy of living, ocean depth of happy rest!
Source of grace and fount of blessing, let your light upon us shine;
teach us how to love each other, lift us to the joy divine.

Mortals join the mighty chorus which the morning stars began;
God's own love is reigning o'er us, joining people hand in hand.
Ever singing, march we onward, victors in the midst of strife;
joyful music leads us sunward in the triumph song of life.

BENEDICTION

SOLO

"Amazing Grace"
Salome Bey
Washington Savage, Piano

RECESSIONAL

ORGAN POSTLUDE

The congregation is invited to the Flora McCrea
Auditorium in the northeast wing of the church for a
reception immediately following the service.

PARTICIPANTS IN TODAY'S SERVICE

The Rev. Dr. Andrew Stirling
Senior Minister

Edward Connell
Organist and Director of Music

Pat Cook
Guitarist

Salome Bey
Soloist

Kollage Jazz Quintet
Archie Alleyne, Drums
Dough Richardson, Tenor Sax
Washington Savage, Piano
Artie Roth, Bass
Alexis Baro, Trumpet

Katherine Sykes
Jennifer Jarvis
Jenny Wood
Readers

Charlotte Carter
Eulogist

APPENDIX F
Readings: Biblical And Other

Old Testament Readings

Job 19.1, 21-27a "I know that my Redeemer
  lives"
Proverbs 31.10-31 "Ode to a capable wife"
Isaiah 25.6-9 "He will swallow up death forever"
Isaiah 61.1-3 "To comfort all who mourn"
Lamentations 3.17-26, 31-33 "The steadfast
  love of the Lord never ceases"
Daniel 12.1-3 "Every one whose name shall be
  found written in the book"
Wisdom 3.1-6, 7-9 "The souls of righteous are
  in the hands of God"

Psalms and Suitable Refrains

23 "The Lord is my shepherd"
25 "Remember me according to your love, O Lord"
27 "The Lord is my light and my salvation"
42 "I will give thanks to him who is my help
  and my God"
46 "God is our refuge and strength"

51 "Have mercy on me, O God, according to your loving kindness"

90 "From age to age you are God"

106 "Praise the Lord! O Give thanks to the Lord, for he is good"

116 "I love the Lord because he has heard my voice and my supplications"

121 "My help comes from the Lord, the maker of heaven and earth"

122 "May they prosper who love Jerusalem"

126 "Those who sowed the tears will reap the songs of joy"

130 "My soul waits for the Lord, for with the Lord there is mercy"

134 "Bless the Lord who made heaven and earth"

139 "Lead me in the way that is everlasting"

150 "Hallelujah! Praise God in His holy temple"

New Testament Readings

Romans 6.3-9 "All of us who were baptized into Christ Jesus were baptized unto his death"

Romans 8.14-19, 34-35, 37-39 "The glory that is to be revealed"

Romans 14.7-9 "Whether we live or whether we die, we are the Lord's"

1 Corinthians 15.20-28, 35-44a "In Christ shall all be made alive"

1 Corinthians 15.50-57 "Death is swallowed up
in victory"

2 Corinthians 4.7-18 "The things that are unseen
are eternal"

2 Corinthians 4.1-9 "What is mortal may be
swallowed up by life"

Philippians 3.20-21 "To be like his glorious
body"

1 Thessalonians 4.13-18 "So we shall always be
with the Lord"

2 Timothy 2.8-12a "If we have died with him,
we shall also live with him"

1 Peter 1.3-9 "We have been born anew to a
living hope"

1 John 3.1-2 "We shall be like him"

1 John 4.7-18a "We may have confidence for
the day of judgment"

Revelation 7.9-17 "God will wipe away every
tear"

Revelation 21.1-7 "Behold I make all things
new"

Gospel Readings

Matthew 5.1-12a "Rejoice and be glad, for your
reward is great in heaven"

Matthew 11.25-30 "Come to me....and I will give
you rest"

Mark 15.33-39 "He has risen, he is not here"

Luke 24.13-16, 17-27, 28-35 "He was known
to them in the breaking of the bread"

John 5. 24-27 "Who hears my word and
believes who sent me, has eternal life"

John 6.37-40 "All that the Father gives me will
come to me"

John 10.11-16 "I am the good shepherd"

John 11.17-27 "I am the resurrection and the
life"

John 14.1-6 "In my Father's house there are
many rooms"

John 20.1-9 "The stone had been taken away
from the tomb"

Ecclesiastes 3.1-9 "For everything there is a
season"

Other Readings

You may want to choose a reading from places
other than the Bible. Here are a few examples of
non-biblical readings. They may be found at your
local library or online.

Anonymous. "You can shed tears that she has
gone," chosen by Queen Elizabeth II to be read
at the Queen Mother's funeral.

Author unknown, "Child of Mine." "I'll lend you for a little while a child of mine..."

Author unknown. "Do not stand at my grave and weep..."

Author unknown. "If I should ever leave you whom I love..."

Auden, W.H. "Stop all the clocks..."

Browning, Elizabeth Barrett. "How do I love thee... I shall but love thee better after death..."

Clements, Donna, "Miss Me But Let Me Go." "When I come to the end of my road..."

Ellis, Linda, "The Dash." "I read of a man who stood to speak..."

Emerson, Ralph Waldo. "To laugh often and much...to win the respect of intelligent people, this is to have succeeded."

Gibran, Kahlil, excerpts from *The Prophet*

Hardy, Thomas, "Regret Me Not." "Regret me not..."

Hitchcock, Colleen, "Ascension." "And if I go while you're still here, know that I live on..."

Holland, Canon Henry Scott. "Death is nothing at all – I have only slipped into the next room."

Hugo, Victor. "Have courage for the great sorrows of life"

Powers, Margaret, "Footprints in the Sand." "One night a man had a dream..."

Richardson, Isla Paschal, "Tender Loving Care." "To those I loved and those who loved me..."

Sharpe, A.L. "Isn't it strange that Princes and Kings..."

Van Dyke, Henry. "Ere thou sleepest, gently lay..."

Van Dyke, Henry. "I am standing on the seashore..."

Wordsworth, William, "Intimations of Immortality." "Though nothing can bring back the hour of splendour in the grass..."

Traditional Gaelic Blessing, "May the road rise up to meet you..."

APPENDIX G
Music

Hymns

United Church Hymnal, *Voices United* (VU)
Anglican Church Hymnal, *Common Praise* (CP)

	VU	CP
Abide With Me	436	24
All People That on Earth Do Dwell Psalm 100	822	349
All Shall Be Well		222
All Things Bright and Beautiful	291	415
Amazing Grace	266	
And I Will Raise You Up on Eagle's Wings	807	531
Battle Hymn of the Republic Onward Christian Soldiers		499
For All the Saints Who from Their Labours Rest	705	276

	VU	CP
Give Thanks for Life	706	
Go Now in Peace	964	
God Be in My Head	430	
Guide Me O Thou Great Jehovah	651	565
I Feel the Winds of God	625	
Jerusalem the Golden		278
Joyful, Joyful We Adore You	232	425
Lift High the Cross	151	602
Lord of the Dance	352	
Now Thank We All Our God	236	399
O God Our Help in Ages Past Psalm 90	806	528
Praise My Soul the God of Heaven	240	381
The Day Thou Gavest	437	29
The Lord Is My Shepherd, Psalm 23	747	519

	VU	CP
The Strife Is O'er, the Battle Done	159	212
Unto the Hills, Psalm 121	842	543
We Are Pilgrims on a Journey	595	
We Hail Thee Now O Jesus		180
What a Friend We Have in Jesus	664	532

Modern Selections

Always on My Mind	Elvis Presley
Candle in the Wind	Elton John
Every Breath You Take	The Police
I Believe	
Morning Has Broken	Cat Stevens
My Country Is My Cathedral	
My Heart Will Go On, Titanic	Celine Dion
My Way	Frank Sinatra

Seasons in the Sun	Terry Jacks
Simply the Best	Tina Turner
Stairway to Heaven	Led Zeppelin
Tears in Heaven	Eric Clapton
Thank You Lord on This Day	Edelweiss
The Wind Beneath My Wings	Bette Midler
Walk Hand in Hand with Me	Andy Williams
Yesterday	The Beatles
You Light Up My Life	Debbie Boone

Christmas Music

Gospel Hymns

Easter Resurrection Hymns

APPENDIX H

The Wake: Things To Remember

Notification

· Put an invitation to the reception in the Order of Service bulletin

· Include a map if necessary

· Invite the minister and the organist

Finger food

· sandwiches, crudités, cheese and crackers, squares, cut-up fruit

· napkins, small plates, and flowers and parsley to decorate the serving trays

Coffee service

· real and decaffeinated coffee, tea, sugar, milk, half and half, lemon slices

· cups and saucers, spoons

Bar (if having)

· red and white wine, beer, liquor, soft drinks and mixes, juices, plain and sparkling water

· glasses (wine, beer, cocktail), ice bucket and ice, tongs, corkscrew, bottle opener, can opener, cocktail napkins,

· garbage receptacle and recycle bin

Buffet dinner (if having)

- casseroles and salads
- dinner plates, serving spoons and salad servers, cutlery wrapped in napkins
- wine, beer, soft drinks and extra glasses
- fresh coffee and squares

BIBLIOGRAPHY AND SUGGESTED READINGS

Agee, James. *A Death in the Family.* New York: Bantam Books, Inc., with Grosset & Dunlop, 1972.

Common Praise. Toronto: Anglican Book Centre, 1998.

Donovan, Daniel. *A Time of Grace.* New Jersey: Paulist Press, 1990.

Kubler-Ross, Elisabeth. *Death: The Final Stage of Growth.* Englewood Cliffs, New Jersey: Prentice-Hall, 1975.

Kushner, Harold S. *When Bad Things Happen to Good People.* New York: Schocken Books, 1985.

Lindbergh, Anne Morrow. *Gift from the Sea.* New York: Vintage Books, 1978.

Martin, John D. *I Can't Stop Crying.* Toronto: Key Porter, 1992.

O'Driscoll, Herbert. *Hope for a Time of Grieving.* Toronto: ABC, 1998.

Post, Peggy. *Emily Post's Etiquette, 16th Edition.*
New York: Collins Publishing Inc.

Schiff, Harriet Sarnoff. *The Bereaved Parent.*
Toronto: Penguin Books, 1981.

Shaw, Eva. *What to Do When a Loved One Dies.*
Dickens Press, 1994.

Simone, Patricia A. *The Complete Funeral Guide.*
Toronto: Gravure-Craft Limited, 1998.

Voices United. Etobicoke, Canada: The United
Church Publishing House, 1996.

Wylie, Betty Jane. *Life's Losses: Living Through
Grief, Bereavement, and Sudden Change.*
Toronto: Macmillan Press, 1996.